UNDERSTANDING
Alternative Political Universes

The Natural Revelation & Self-Evident Truths

Frank N. Mitchell

This UNDERSTANDING booklet is part of a series of booklets on key issues of our time on the Reign of Christ at
www.ashiningcityonahill.org
www.reignofchrist.org
All booklets are available at amazon.com

September 2018

UNDERSTANDING
Alternative Political Universes
The Natural Revelation &
Self-Evident Truths

We in America today and in the two political parties seem to live in alternative moral, political, and even worldview universes. But why is this? It is because Democrats and Republicans have different self-evident truths. The Declaration of Independence holds famously "We hold these truths to be self-evident that all men are created equal endowed by their creator with certain inalienable rights, among them life, liberty, and the pursuit of happiness."

A foundational point of **both** Liberalism and atheism is a rejection of these self-evident truths. However, the entire point of the Declaration of Independence is that separation from Great Britain was justified because of the injustices the colonists saw Britain to have done to them in violation of the moral "Laws of Nature and of Nature's God." The central point here is if there is no Higher Moral Law, then there is no real, valid or just reason for the Americans to seek an independent, separate and equal status as a nation.

Self-evident truths but for whom?
Self-evident truths in geometry are truths that do not have to be proved or deduced. They are known to people self-evidently by common sense or, that is to

say, by the sense we all have in common by virtue of our humanity and God-given natural reason.

Tragically, this common sense of natural reason can be lost. (See Romans 1 & 2 and 2 Timothy 3.) When this loss of common sense occurs things that once seemed self-evident, obvious, and good no longer do, and this can also be true of Jefferson's self-evident truths in the Declaration of Independence. Traditionally, in Western civilization there are seen to be two ways that we as human beings come to know things. One way is basic **natural reason** about life, nature, morality, justice, righteousness, and the universe. This is sometimes called the Natural Revelation. The second way we know things about these subjects is because **the Bible** (God's inspired Word) says something is so. The Bible is sometimes called the Special Revelation.

In centuries past in Western civilization, which now outside of Islam has generally become world civilization, God has been seen to use these two Revelations to create all knowledge for all mankind on Earth. The ancient Greeks and Romans were the first to develop natural reason and natural knowledge in a systematic manner. And in reality almost all the structure and substance of modern natural thinking traces back to its beginnings in ancient Athens with our modern science being something of an exception, though the beginning roots of modern science also trace back to some degree to ancient

Athens where philosophers tried to think in a systematic way about the natural world.

With the Special Revelation of the Bible given directly from God, things are known to be true simply because God says so through the many believed to be divinely inspired writers of the Bible text. This is said to be the tradition that comes out of Jerusalem. As is well-known in the early centuries of the church, these two Revelations were merged by the early Christians, and the merger created, in essence, what we today call the Western tradition, and that merger actually happened immediately in the early church in the New Testament when Paul and others went to the Gentile world to preach the Gospel.

What is the Good News of the Gospel? Christ died on the Cross for our sins in order to give us new life in the Spirit of God in this life and so we could avoid the Final Judgment of God and go to heaven for all eternity in the next life. Revelation 21 actually indicates there will be a new heaven and new earth. In short, in Christianity all men have sinned and fallen short of the glory of God and need a Savior, and all men are spiritually dead from Adam's fall and need to be born again of the Spirit in Christ.

There is nothing complicated here, but Paul had several problems in preaching the Gospel to the Gentiles. One problem is that, as Scripture says, Satan can somehow blind people to the glorious light of the Gospel. (See 2 Corinthians 4:4.) In truth, most people who hear the Gospel and have no mental confusion or blindness from demonic spirits and have no hardened heart will usually accept it. I mean why would one not accept it? Paul found the answer to why some people do not accept the Gospel is that some people have a conscience as seared with a hot iron and, therefore, they do not accept the fact they are sinners or have ever sinned in the first place in order to need a Savior in the second place.

The key point here is the Gentiles did **not** have the Law of Moses that states explicitly what sin is, such as breaking the Ten Commandments. So Paul says when he preaches the Gospel to the Gentiles he appeals to their natural conscience (2 Corinthians 4:2) that they are sinners and not to the Law of Moses, as such. However, Paul says some people have in fact lost their natural conscience and in essence their common sense and their natural affections and so forth. For these people there is no real right and wrong in the nature of things (self-evidently) in order for there to be any real sin. Further, for these same people there is absolutely nothing about life that makes them think there is a God, they say themselves. For them in the Natural Revelation the heavens do **not** declare the glory of God and the firmament his workmanship or craftsmanship, etc. But, as the Bible says, it is **only** the exceptional fool who says in his heart there is no God and who says what is self-evident foolishness and moral depravity to common sense for most of the rest of mankind.

What does this mean? Paul found that natural man generally tends to think there is a God because of the majesty of the creation and because of his natural conscience and similar things, but some few folks have a hardened heart, a seared conscience, and a defiled mind, and they do not see the slightest evidence for God in life or the creation. In short, they believe there is no Creator God, and there is no real right and wrong. This position is called atheism or agnosticism and moral depravity, and it had philosophical schools associated with it dealing with the Natural Revelation in the ancient Greco-Roman world.

The Epicureans
The ancient atheist philosophical schools were those such as the Sophists, the Cynics, and most centrally and importantly, the Epicureans. For these thinkers it is quite clear to them and **quite self-evident to them that all men are *not* created equal *nor* endowed by their Creator with certain inalienable rights, among them life, liberty, and the pursuit of happiness, and there are certainly and self-evidently *no* moral Laws of Nature and Nature's God**. This means the very two things that are **self-evidently true** to most natural men (namely, that there is a Creator God and a real right and wrong called the Higher Moral Law) are **self-evidently**

false to these morally depraved people, the Epicureans.

The Epicureans live, quite indisputably, in an alternative universe of self-evident truths, for better or worse. The problem that emerged in the ancient Greco-Roman world is that the morally depraved atheists (in particular the Epicureans) were convinced that they had figured out the true "nature of things" and that the vast majority of people who believed by natural reason in a real Creator God and a real right and wrong were idiots, unenlightened, uneducated, etc., because the average man is not smart enough, educated enough or enlightened enough to see there is obviously no real God and no real right and wrong, and this was self-evident for them.

Two Competing Worldviews

So, in the ancient world prior to the time of Christianity there were two basic competing worldviews. One said, more or less, as the Sophists, Cynics, and Epicureans that there is *no* God and *no* real right and wrong (moral laws of nature) and no life after death and no judgment of sin after death. And the other group of thinkers most famously Heraclitus, Socrates, Plato, Aristotle, and Cicero held that natural reason or Natural Revelation says there is a God and a real right and wrong and possibly, even probably, a life after death, and, if so, probably a judgment of sin after death. And it is from this second group of people culminating in Cicero that we get the ideas that all men are created equal (before God) and endowed by their Creator with certain inalienable rights and that there are real moral Laws of Nature and of Nature's God. In fact, it is in these ancient thinkers where all these ideas of Locke and Jefferson started for what will become Western civilization.

What happens in the ancient world with the rise of Christianity as it spreads throughout the Roman Empire is the Early Church Fathers step into the debate and the battle of the two basic worldviews and the battle between the Sophists, Cynics, and Epicureans (basically hedonist atheists) *versus* thinkers like Heraclitus, Socrates, Plato, Aristotle, and Cicero (basically moral theists), and the Christians say the second group of people are obviously correct in their thinking about the nature of things. And they are not just self-evidently correct, but they are also correct because they line up with the clear teaching of Scripture concerning the Natural Revelation.

The Early Church Fathers as Justin, Origen, and Augustine are some of the greatest minds that ever existed, and they turn all of their intellectual firepower on the thinkers such as the Epicureans, the Gnostics, and eventually the Neo-Platonists, all of whom hold there is no real Creator God and no real right and wrong. This makes for great reading to this very day because the Early Church Fathers blow their opponents out of the water as being morally depraved atheist fools if not faulty mystics of some sort, and in doing so, they create **the Western tradition** that says there are the two forms of knowledge, namely, the Natural Revelation which says to all but fools and the morally depraved that there is a real Creator God and a real Higher Moral Law in the nature of things, and further, there is a second form of knowledge which is the Special Revelation, the Bible, that tells us about the real, specific and special covenant in Christ that God entered into with all mankind at the Cross where Christ died for our sins.

The Philosophes
There was some minor questioning of the Western tradition in the Renaissance but little serious questioning until the 18th century humanist Enlightenment, which for variety of reasons decided the Western tradition of the previous 1700 years was all wrong. These atheist, morally depraved Enlightenment thinkers actually had a name. They were called the Philosophes, and their views were an open attempt to bring back the false, foolish and morally depraved self-evident "truths" of the ancient Epicureans with no God, no Higher Moral Law, and no life after death, and often for some of them there was even no realm of the spirit or mind. Man was simply a physical pleasure-calculus machine.

That is to say, as with the ancient Epicureans, most of these atheist thinkers were outright materialists, which, in fact, is a self-evident laughably absurd position, and further they held with virtually no argument whatsoever that the entire Bible was a book of mythology and superstition. And, as in the ancient world before Christianity came on the scene, these Philosophe thinkers in their revival of Epicureanism thought they were smarter than everyone else and smarter than the ordinary man who still believed in a Creator God and a Higher Moral Law and in a Savior who died on the Cross for our sins so we could avoid the Final Judgment and be made right or reconciled to God and have Jesus dwell in our hearts.

This means for the Philosophes except for empirical science the whole prior, noble, and inspiring Western tradition of the Natural and Special Revelations was thrown to the wind as **self-evident** foolishness, superstition, and nonsense, and hence, for the most part these people did this for no valid reason whatsoever. This was, in fact, a recreation of the ancient discredited alternative universe of the Epicureans that these Enlightenment thinkers lived in while thinking they were on the cutting edge of progress, and they felt they were justified in this moral depravity and loss of traditional common sense because of the rise of modern science.

Roughly speaking, the Copernican Revolution placing the sun at the center of the solar system and the discovery of gravity by the brilliant Sir Issac Newton supposedly proved conclusively there is no God, no Higher Moral Law and no realm of the spirit or of mind and no mental truth. This is not only outrageous silliness, but is a conclusion that Newton himself never dreamed of coming to but that did not deter these modern day Epicureans who thought they were smarter than everyone else and were convinced, in essence, that Newton in the end was also an idiot and did not understand the significance of his own work! They, of course, do not outright, to my knowledge, call Newton himself an idiot, but they make the most ruthless attacks imaginable on the bulk of mankind who do not accept that Newton's modern science supposedly conclusively proves ancient atheist morally depraved Epicureanism to be completely valid, vindicated and self-evidently true concerning the Natural Revelation, and if this is the case, the Bible cannot possibly be true.

This makes for two types of political revolutions
Bertrand Russell and H. G. Wells are two of the most famous advocates of this above analysis, and as atheists they think this transition into ancient Epicureanism and this collapse of Western civilization (concerning both the Natural and Special Revelations) is a good thing and not a bad thing, and understandably so since they are modern day Epicureans. What does this mean?

The issue that is going to emerge primarily in the UK (but also eventually the US) is not did this collapse into ancient Epicureanism happen, but is it a good thing or a bad thing and whose universe is to be seen as the true, good and self-evident one? The foolish morally depraved materialist-atheists will think this bringing back of ancient Epicureanism is a good thing, and those people who believe in a real Creator God and a real Higher Moral Law and a real Savior who died for their sins will think it is a bad thing.

And, as is well-known, things get very dicey in the 18th century politically with two famous political revolutions. In 1776 in America there is a revolution based on the moral "Laws of Nature and of Nature's God," and eventually it turns out to be probably the most wonderful thing to ever happen in history politically, though in fact it is primarily a republican version of the 1688 Glorious Revolution, and both of these revolutions were based on the teachings of John Locke and on the moral Laws of Nature and of Nature's God, which are self-evidently absurd to the modern Epicureans. So, in 1789 in France there was also a revolution, but it was based on the hedonist Epicurean teachings of the Philosophes and not based on the moral Laws of Nature and of Nature's God, and things did not turn out so well with the French Revolution with its infamous reign of terror when thousands get their heads cut off!

The French revolutionaries had a rallying cry of "Liberty, Equality, and Fraternity," but they actually had no worked out theory of these terms and understandably so with their rejection of the Higher Moral Law, but basically they wanted Liberty from the oppressive monarchy and aristocracy, and they wanted Equality with the aristocracy, and they wanted Fraternity among the bourgeois middle class, but not with the proletariat working class. And in the end, for these revolutionaries might makes right if there is no Higher Moral Law of the Laws of Nature and of Nature's God.

In short, the British Glorious Revolution of 1688 and the America Revolution of 1776 were based on the moral Laws of Nature and of Nature's God while the French Revolution of 1789 was based on the morally depraved, laughably absurd alternative universe of the hedonist, might-makes-right Epicureans. Further, as many people have pointed out over the years, the American Revolution was technically no revolution at all since it was a war for independence and not a war to overthrow the British government itself. Basically the American colonists held that their rights as Englishmen, established in the Glorious Revolution of 1688, were not being respected.

So, both the British Glorious Revolution of 1688 and the America Revolution of 1776 believed in traditional concepts of Justice, Righteousness, private property, free enterprise, consent of the governed, and equal rights for all, and they believed in freedom of speech, press, and religion, and most important of all, they believed in free sovereign states, but virtually every one of these things are (or become) laughably absurd ideas and laughably absurd self-evident truths and goods in the alternative universe of the modern day Epicurean, who is a materialist, hedonist, humanist, might-makes-right atheist. Karl Marx is such an atheist, and for Marx in his nutty alternative Epicurean universe, everything is turned on its head as self-evident truths and goods.

Marx is an outspoken, laughably absurd materialist atheist for whom there is self-evidently no realm of the mind or spirit and for whom Justice, Righteousness, private property, free enterprise, consent of the governed, equal rights for all, freedom of speech, press, and religion, and free sovereign states are *not* goods. And **seeing these things as *not* good or true is for the Epicurean Marxist the height of brilliance, enlightenment, and education especially concerning matters of economics and government.** But as Ronald Reagan correctly said, Marxism is not a form of economics, it is a "form of insanity" where in an alternative universe slavery and tyranny are self-evident goods and where Liberty and Justice for all are self-evident evils!!!

Marxism makes for a true dehumanizing dystopia. In Marxism free enterprise, private property, and all individual rights must be eliminated by a violent might-makes-right revolution of the proletariat class against the capitalist bourgeoisie middle class in order to eliminate the supposed (self-evident) evils of private property, free enterprise, all individual rights and liberties, and so forth, and ultimately all nation-states.

Socialist Democrats and their false "third way" Social Justice

What happens in the late 19th century is there are Epicureans, primarily in the UK, who are, in part, highly offended by this **violent** revolution agenda of Marx pitting class against class in violent conflict, but they are for the most part still on board for the laughably absurd positions of the hedonist, humanist, materialist-atheist Epicureans, and so they also hold as Marx had held that classical concepts of Justice, Righteousness, private property, free enterprise, most individual rights, and free sovereign states are self-evident evils in their alternative **non-violent** Epicurean universe.

So, these hedonist Epicurean atheists become non-violent communist collectivists, and they call their position a "third way," which, in fact, was a second-way communism. They are generally utopian pacifist collectivists, but **they want to set up the same communist state that Marx sought to set up** but these utopian communists want to set up their communist state by the ballot box and not by violent class revolution, and they want their collectivist communist state to be based on a false "moral" principle of the universal brotherhood of man and not on might makes right as Marx had held. Marx had wanted to set up a tyrannical communism of the "dictatorship of the proletariat" where all people in the world work in slave labor for subsistence wages under a tyrannical one-world government and where there are zero rights and freedoms for any individuals in a truly insane worldwide dystopia.

However, the utopian communists call themselves "social democrats" because they believe in socialism by democracy or voting (not by violence) to set up a one-world socialist government to redistribute all the world's wealth and resources equally to all people since we are all equally one of the universal brotherhood of man, and therefore everyone supposedly has an equal right to an equal share of the world's wealth and resources whether one works or not. Working does not add to that right for an equal share, and not working does not take away from that right to an equal share of the world's wealth. When one gets one's equal share, that is called Socialist Justice or Social Justice. In this utopian socialism no one will have to work at all, and all work will be voluntary with no pay check because the **new socialist man** does all work in **selfless service to the collective**.

This **selfless service to the collective** is because, as in hard Marxism, any self-interest or any individuality is a self-evident evil, even if the self-interest is legitimate or moral. Indeed, as with Epicureanism generally, all classical concepts of Justice and Righteousness are self-evidently evil and/or just plain non-existent. And, further, with the new single false moral standard of "the universal brotherhood of man" classical concepts of Justice and Righteousness are particularly bad being bigoted, prejudiced, and divisive because they violate the utopian unity of the family of man and his brotherhood, etc.

In this utopian socialism by democracy there will be freedom of speech, press, and religion, but it cannot speak the truth about anything dealing with divisive Justice and Righteousness because that is hate speech. So, freedom of speech, press, and religion exists in name only because one is only free to be politically correct, which is no freedom at all! And there is also a false agape love in this utopian socialism, and it is called "unconditional love," and it is a utopian agape love as lawlessness, much as the ancient Gnostics had. So, the apostate churches (apostate to the "fundamentals" of the Christian faith) embrace a universal fatherhood of God (of unconditional love), and they *also* embrace the same universal brotherhood of man (as the so-called "third way" communists), and the apostate Christians generally hold everybody goes to heaven because of their false "God" and his false unconditional love where no atoning sacrifice is needed, etc.

Three universes to live in
So, this now gives us three universes to live in: First, there is Liberty and Justice for all and equal rights for all based on the moral Laws of Nature and of Nature's God, which are self-evident to common sense. Second, there is a violent dystopian communism of Marx with no individual rights (to property, free enterprise, speech, press, religion, etc.)

and with no Liberty and Justice for anybody. Third, in what will come to be known as "the third way," there is non-violent utopian communism of the social democrats doing worldwide communism in the name of Social Justice and its so-called positive rights to an equal share of the world's wealth based on the false moral principle of the universal brotherhood of man and voluntary selfless service to the collective.

This hedonist Epicurean "third way" and one-world government are to be established by voting for this supposedly morally superior utopian communist collectivism based on the universal brotherhood of man and his socialist positive "human rights" to an equal share, etc. And these socialist democrats say this will supposedly do the greatest good for the greatest number by seizing the wealth of the top 30% and handing it out to the bottom 70% to make us all equal in worldwide "Social Justice" socialism, where no one has to work a day in their lives. (This will be the perfect utopia, if we can just "imagine" it and vote for it and its Social Justice, etc.)

This redistribution means 70% of people will think they stand to gain in this utopian, hedonist, socialist New World Order, and they will have the comfort of thinking they are doing the morally right thing in so voting. And they will even think they are being morally superior in so voting because the social democrats come up with a plan to teach in all the schools and churches the supposedly desirable and self-evident truth of Epicurean hedonism and its moral depravity along with its single utopian false moral standard of the universal brotherhood of man with its supposed good of agape love as lawlessness. This is done in the churches by adding the universal fatherhood of God to the false moral standard of the social democrats, namely, the universal brotherhood of man, which is to be taught in all the schools.

So, in all the schools and all the churches you repeat over and over and over again the new politically correct truth for the schools and the new catechism for the churches as supposedly self-evident truths in an alternative universe of the socialist democrats. The teacher in the pc schools and the preacher in the pc apostate churches have essentially the same curriculum. It is as follows:

"Please repeat after me: the nation-state is a self-evident evil and causes wars, and global socialist government is a self-evident good and prevents wars. Open borders and open immigration are self-evident goods, and borders, walls, and the rule of law are self-evident evils. Unconditional love and agape love as lawlessness, license and indulgence are goods, and traditional love of common sense and the Bible are self-evident evils. Radical multiculturalism and Social Justice are self-evident goods, and traditional Justice and Righteousness are self-evident evils, and traditional Justice and Righteousness are bigoted, prejudiced, hateful, and intolerant. Transgendered homosexuality is self-evidently moral and good, and straight heterosexuality is self-evidently abnormal, unloving, homophobic, and evil. National citizenship and identity are also self-evident evils, and they are also bigoted, prejudiced, intolerant and xenophobic, but being a citizen of the one-world government is a self-evident good. Democratic populism is a self-evident evil, and being ruled by a small tyrannical unelected globalist elite is a self-evident good. Free enterprise, private property, and all traditional individual rights and freedoms are self-evident evils, and collectivism and positive human rights for hedonistic indulgence and an equal share of the world's wealth are self-evident goods. And if there is a God it is self-evident truth that all religions worship the same God but by a different name, and it is a self-evident evil to say Jesus is the only way to a restored relationship to the God who created the entire universe and everything in it. Anyone who agrees with these self-evident truths and goods is a good person and is truly enlightened and truly well-educated, and anyone who does not agree with these new self-evident truths is a deplorable, bigoted, prejudiced, uneducated, unenlightened, politically incorrect idiot and should be fined, imprisoned or socially ostracized."

For these Epicurean social democrats with their false agape love and Socialist Justice, the point of life is self-evidently hedonistic self-indulgence and a false inclusion, and not moral virtue. And the point of religion is spiritual experiences of tolerance, compassion, and oneness with the non-existent "God" of all religions and not spiritual experiences of the Abba Father relationship with the perfectly Righteous and Loving God who created the whole universe and sent his Son to die on the Cross for the sins all mankind in order to restore what had been lost in Adam's fall.

Bottom line: outright evil, false goods, and true goods

In the alternative universe of the hedonist-Epicurean utopian socialist up is down and good is bad, just as Isaiah said (Isaiah 5:20) of a society in such decline and in absurd depravity, but with the "third way" social democrat it is in the name of "love" and "brotherhood" and "inclusion" and not in the name of hatred, violence, and class conflict as Marx had done in his communism. Getting caught up in this politically correct, upside-down Orwellian nonsense as today's Liberals, atheists and globalists do is known in the Bible as demonic "ensnarement" in "doctrines of demons," which one comes to think are brilliant and good and even moral, but they are, in fact, self-evidently absurd, morally depraved, and even evil to traditional common sense. (See 1 Timothy 4:1 and 2 Timothy 2:24-26.)

The key to understanding how everything went wrong in Western civilization with the Judeo-Christian worldview being trashed is to see that the violent, dehumanizing, dystopian communism of Marx was an outright evil that Marx called good, just as Hitler's national socialism of the Nazi Party was an outright evil that he called good. However, the utopian, non-violent socialism of the social democrats in the name of a false brotherly agape love is *also* a demonic deception, but it is more a false or counterfeit good than an outright evil.

Though Social Justice and false agape love as lawlessness are not outright evils, as such, the end result is basically the same as the old Marxism, namely, an Epicurean hedonism for personal living or an inclusion or tolerance of it as a supposedly self-evident good, and there is to be a communist state with no real Liberty and Justice for anybody and, hence, no real rights and freedoms for anybody at least as traditionally defined. All of this is done by social democrats as the new self-evident goods. This is the surreal and upside-down Alice-in-Wonderland world of today's Democrat Party in the US and today's Labour Party in the UK. This politically correct world is as George Orwell's novel *1984* where everything is seen as its opposite.

In truth, **Social Justice** with its positive entitlement rights to an equal share of the world's wealth is **the opposite** of **classical Justice** where one deserves the fruits of one's own labors.

Social Justice is simply a phony moral justification for a worldwide communism and tyranny by today's globalists. And once people see these demonic deceptions and false goods for what they are, they will be exposed and defeated in all the schools, all the churches, all the media and in all politics forever, and at that time Liberty and Justice for all in free sovereign states with consent of the governed and equal rights for all based on the moral Laws of Nature and of Nature's God Wisely applied by the statesman legislator for the common good or general welfare of the nation will be seen once again as self-evidently true, good, and desirable, just as the Glorious Revolution and American Revolution held.

===

Other booklets on the Reign of Christ in this UNDERSTANDING Series:

UNDERSTANDING Prophecy Fulfillment:
The Great Apostasy, Babylon, Mystery Babylon & the Reign of Christ

This little booklet gives an overview of the central major prophecies concerning the possible soon coming Reign of Christ. Specifically these are the prophecies of the Great Apostasy, Babylon, Mystery Babylon, and the man of lawlessness. These prophecies are seen as fulfilled in the false millennial visions of Marx and of the New World Order of UN Agenda 21 and Agenda 2030 and in the Liberal World Council of Churches.

UNDERSTANDING All Bible Prophecy:
Genesis to Revelation

This booklet holds that all prophecy should be interpreted in terms of the larger story of the Bible and the larger story of the Christian cosmology from the Creation to the Final Judgment, and this is especially the case for the book of Revelation.

UNDERSTANDING Globalism:
What is the "New World Order"?

This booklet looks at what "globalism" is generally and at the related topic of a "New World Order" that actually has *very* specific definitions and formulations that are often not well-known.

UNDERSTANDING Revelation 19:
Victory over One-World Government and One-World Religion

Revelation 19 though very controversial is actually very straightforward. The saints in a Marriage Supper of the Lamb move into a new more mature, intimate, and complete relationship with Christ, and then the saints in Christ and Christ in the saints completely and totally defeat the evils of one-world government and one-world religion. Simple enough when you get right down to it.

UNDERSTANDING Statesmanship
Classical Justice *versus* Social Justice

Probably no two notions are more misunderstood as well as more necessary to understand in our time than classical Justice and Social Justice. This booklet looks at the history of these two terms and how one stands for the Justice of statesmanship for doing the common good and the other for the injustice of special interest groups and wealth redistribution as a false human right for economic equality.

UNDERSTANDING Alternative Political Universes:
The Natural Revelation & Self-Evident Truths

For some folks as Jefferson and the American founders, the Natural Law or so-called Higher Moral Law is a self-evident truth, but for others with a reprobate mind and no common sense, this is not the case at all. These modern-day people who have lost their common sense are just as the ancient Epicureans (atheist hedonists) while modern-day Liberals are just as ancient Gnostics with their false enlightenment and false morality. Understand these things, and you will pretty well understand Alternative Political Universes.

UNDERSTANDING Illegal Immigration:
The Wall and All It Stands For

"The Wall" of Donald Trump stands for many larger issues from exposing hypocrisy among professional politicians to ending globalism, open borders, and the often total lawlessness of our time. Lawlessness of the Liberal and atheist-humanist is, in fact, the spirit of anti-Christ.

UNDERSTANDING The Whole Counsel of the Kingdom:
The Central Message of Jesus and Paul

Both Jesus and Paul preached a Whole Counsel of the Kingdom message, but this is not a generally well-known truth. This booklet looks at the concept of a Whole Counsel of the Kingdom Christianity and what it entails, namely, true worship of God in Spirit and Truth as well as Just and Righteous government.

UNDERSTANDING Spiritual Warfare:
Satan as a Roaring Lion

Scripture tells us that Satan goes about like a roaring lion seeking whom he may devour, but this is generally not a very understood warning, and tragically many people, if not devoured completely, get an arm or leg eaten (so to speak). To be forewarned is to be forearmed. This booklet deals with ways to recognize and deal with demons.

===

All of the above booklets are part of a series on key issues of our time on the Reign of Christ at
www.ashiningcityonahill.org
www.reignofchrist.org

All of the above booklets are put together is a single **Volume I** called

UNDERSTANDING
The Reign of CHRIST
The One Big Issue of Our Time
Volume I

This Volume I of all the above booklets together as well as all of the above booklets separately are available at **amazon.com**

www.ingramcontent.com/pod-product-compliance
Lightning Source LLC
Chambersburg PA
CBHW061327250726

48657CB00003B/1085